NICK BUTTERWORTH AND MICK INKPEN

THE TWO SONS

Northumberland Schools Library Service	
3 0132 02005570 8	
Askews	Jan-2011
S225 PINK	£3.99

CANDLE
BOOKS

To help people understand what God is like,
Jesus told lots of stories which are as exciting
today as when they were first heard.

The Two Sons is still a great favourite
and its message is one that children especially
love to hear.

This edition published by Candle Books in 2008,
a publishing imprint of Lion Hudson plc.

Distributed in the UK by Marston Book Services Ltd,
PO Box 269, Abingdon, Oxon OX14 4YN

Text and illustrations copyright © 1986, 1989 Nick Butterworth and Mick Inkpen.
First published by Marshall, Morgan & Scott.
Nick Butterworth and Mick Inkpen assert the moral right to be identified as the
authors and illustrators of this work.

Scripture quotations in this book are taken from the Good News Bible © 1966, 1971,
1976, 1992 American Bible Society.

All rights reserved. No part of this publication may be reproduced, stored in a
retrieval system, or transmitted in any form or by any means – electronic,
mechanical, photocopy, recording, or any other – except for brief quotations in
printed reviews, without the prior written permission of the publisher.

International publishing rights owned by Zondervan®.
Worldwide co-edition produced by Lion Hudson plc,
Wilkinson House, Jordan Hill Road, Oxford, OX2 8DR
Tel: +44 (0)1865 302750 Fax: +44 (0)1865 302757
Email: coed@lionhudson.com www.lionhudson.com

ISBN 978 1 85985 748 9

Printed in China

NICK BUTTERWORTH AND MICK INKPEN

THE TWO SONS

Here is a man.

He grows apples in an orchard.

The apples are red and rosy.
It is time for them to be picked.

At home the man has two sons.

'I want you to help me to pick the apples,' says the man to his first son.

'No,' says the first son. 'I'm busy.'

But after a while he is sorry
for what he said.

He picks up a basket and goes
to the orchard.

The man finds his second son.

'I want you to help me pick the apples too,' he says.

'Yes,' says the second son.
'I will come as soon as I have
put on my boots.'

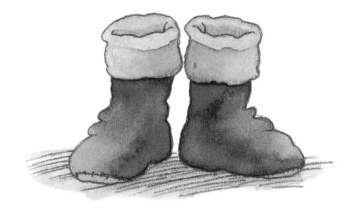

Back in the orchard the first son is busy picking apples.

Look, he has already filled one basket.

'Well done, son,' says the man.
'Here is another basket.
We'll have this done in no time.'

They work together until all
the apples have been picked.
But there is no sign of the
second son.

He has forgotten his promise.

Who do you think pleased his father?

The first son or the second son?

Jesus says,
'What we do is
more important
than what
we say.'

Jesus said, 'Now what do you think?
There was once a man who had two sons. He went to the elder
one and said, "Son, go and work in the vineyard today." "I don't
want to," he answered, but later he changed his mind and went.
Then the father went to the other son and said the same thing.
"Yes, sir," he answered, but he did not go. Which one of the two
sons did what his father wanted?'

Matthew 21:28–31

Other titles from **Candle Books** *by*
Nick Butterworth and Mick Inkpen

The House On The Rock
The Lost Sheep
The Precious Pearl
The Good Stranger
The Two Sons
The Rich Farmer
The Ten Silver Coins
The Little Gate

Stories Jesus Told
Animal Tales
Stories Jesus Told Colouring Book